ART OF CANCER

ALSO BY MARGARET CROUSE SKELLY

POETRY

The Girl in the Orange Dress

ART OF CANCER

MARGARET CROUSE SKELLY

Copyright © 2014 Margaret Crouse Skelly
All rights reserved.

FIRST EDITION Printed in U.S.A.

Cover design by Conrad Warre.

Author photograph by Jill Goldman. www.jillgoldman.com

Cover image, "DNA Research of Science Genetic Data Background" Copyright © shutterstock/kentoh, reprinted with permission.

ISBN 978-148232539

This book is dedicated to my family, friends and caregivers.
With deepest gratitude for . . .

. . . the love and support of my family.
George, Caroline, William and Tao (woof!)
George, Tony, Michael & Lori, Bonnie & Manny, Mark & Trishia, Matty & Sarah

. . . my medical dream team at the Massachusetts General Hospital
Dr. Alice Shaw
Dr. Elizabeth Stover
Dr. Jennifer Shin
Dr. Henning Willers
Dr. William Brugge
Dr. Christopher Morse
Pamela Connolly
Cynthia Moore, Ph.D.
Kristin Anderson
Helen Brandt

. . . my inner circle
Dr. Geetanjali Akerkar
Mary Charnley
Ronda Goldberg
Jill Goldman
Margie Harrigan
Brenda Hicks
Joanna Quinlan
Chuck Smith
Ann Spindler
Bernie Svedlow

. . . my Grace Chapel family, Lexington, Massachusetts
Pastor Bryan Wilkerson and Karen Wilkerson
Nancy ("Chief") and Larry Babine, Laura Crosby and all of my LC Friends
Brigitte Senkler and all of my friends in the women's group
Princess Eliza

. . . the hundreds of friends in my lotsahelpinghands.com community of helpers

With special thanks for making this book happen
Tena Herlihy
Emily Rubin
Lorraine Ward
Nancy West

FOREWARD

On June 6, 2011, I was first diagnosed with Stage 3 adenocarcinoma of the esophagus. My only symptom was difficulty swallowing. I was 48 years old, and otherwise healthy. This devastating diagnosis set off a whirlwind treatment of intense chemotherapy, daily radiation, and ultimately, a major surgery where most of my esophagus and part of my stomach was removed.

Cancer changes everything. It bisects your life. There is your life before cancer, and then there is your life after cancer. And if you are reading this and have cancer, I hope that your life after diagnosis is a very long one.

I have written poetry since I was a teenager, and during my treatment, I wrote to process the emotions I felt as a cancer patient. It was cathartic, and also a way to share my journey with family and friends.

After two years of being NED ("No Evidence of Disease"), my cancer recurred in January 2014, this time in my bones. I am living with cancer. I am Stage 4 now, and in perpetual treatment. When my cancer recurred, I continued to chronicle my story, and the result is this book, which I wrote to reach out to other cancer patients, to survivors, to caregivers, to grievers. My hope is that some of these poems will resonate with you, that you will nod, yes, yes, I have felt that, too.

I also wish to open a dialogue about cancer. Many people have told me they don't know what to say when someone they know has cancer, so they say nothing. My hope is that talking about what it's like to live with cancer will bring comfort to you.

Margaret Crouse Skelly
November 2014
Boston, Massachusetts

Contents

I.

RECEIVING DIAGNOSIS   2

CANCER IS A BLESSING   3

CHOKING   4

JULIA'S SCARF   5

GOIN' TO WALMART WITH MY PARTY DRESS ON   6

MARY SUNSHINE   7

GOOD TIMING   8

NEED   9

WAITING FOR SURGERY   10

RULES OF FORGETTING   11

FEAR OF FAILURE   12

GET OVER THIS GIRL   13

CANCER BUDDIES   14

RECURRENCE   15

PARADOX   16

GUILTING THE LILY   17

MARY, MARY   18

WHAT I WANT YOU TO KNOW   19

HEALING   21

YOUR SIX WORD STORY   22

GARBAGE TOWN   23

II.

GETTING PAST WORDS AGAIN   25

I'M PISSED OFF   26

NEW LOVE SONG FOR THE OLD (HAPPY VALENTINE'S DAY 2014 TO GEORGE FROM MARGARET)   27

STRAWBERRIES IN THE MAILBOX   28

FIDELITY   29

PATIENT   30

NOT WILLIAM, NOT CAROLINE   31

LETTING GO   32

AFFINITIES   33

DIVERSIONS   34

HOLES IN THE HEART   35

SIGNS   36

CHARLES STREET REPAIRS   37

THANK YOU, MRS. FLOWERS   38

ON NOT BEING GOOD ENOUGH MOST DAYS   39

FRIENDS AND SHIPS   40

ON MAUI   41

REUNION   42

LAUGH TRACK   43

CELLS   44

VULNERABILITY   45

TURNING CORNERS   46

HOLDING ELIZA   47

I DIDN'T DO ANYTHING WRONG   48

RAINBOW HAIKUS   49

MENISCUS IN THE BEAKER   50

I.

RECEIVING DIAGNOSIS

Hallways receive us
like the arms of an old friend,

like the feel of the bicycle balance
after long absence from the saddle.

We can't quite crystallize the familiarity
as we navigate the maze so deftly.

Why does this somber feel wrong here,
the smell of hospital coffee numbing, not gut-wrenching.

Then memory slams me.
As the couple turns and approaches,

her swollen belly like the sun rising
round the corner.

The last time we were here:
to bring new life, our son.

How we held him skin-to-skin,
drunk on baby scent,

staring the memory of new face
into our brains.

It's been eight years now.
We anchor into each other, brace ourselves.

CANCER IS A BLESSING

When you get the news,
you are floating.
There is disbelief.
The cancer lifts your friends to the surface.
Some fall away.
But mostly, they cling to you.
You are lucky for this buoy.

There is God like never before.
So close you can feel his breath
as he whispers in your ear.

There is the blue hydrangea in your garden.
Every morning the miracle of new blooms.
Spectacular.
You had never noticed.

There is your son.
You see him for the hundredth-millionth time.
God, he is gorgeous.
All those cells assembled to perfection.
You need to touch his cheek.

There is your daughter,
quietly hoarding a secret nugget of wit.
You yearn to hold her infant bundle again.

There are lovers, friends, and brothers.
You embrace the urge to tell them,
I love you,
This raw truth, it makes you ache.

Each day you lie on the radiation table.
You see the cancer cells taking their leave
with each pulse of light energy.
You promise to be diligent in the moment,
every moment, as you say your goodbyes.

There is faith.
Nothing else.
You tell yourself, *Love.*

CHOKING

The thing about my cancer is this:
the esophagus is not superfluous.
Except when inserting foot
in exchange for sputter.

Or, according to my kids,
when used to honk and wail.
No, definitely, no usefulness in gullet
as old yeller.
I quietly concede their point here.

I mean no disrespect for the breast
or its holy place in our culture, or my marriage, even,
or its beauty in any form, bountiful or not,
or its priceless sentimental value to you, or you.
I, too, believe in the wholeness of body as temple,
flawed or perfect, shrine.

It's simply that I know this truth:
love survives the carving of breast,
body survives the scarring of tissue.

But the esophagus lacks cachet.
The very word congeals on the tongue.
Unless.

Delicately swaddled in bolts of silken tissue,
a princess cached for smuggling out,
long-stemmed Easter lily throat of a dancer,
tender receptacle to land a kiss or caress.

True, the throat can be extraneous.

But I'm getting at something deeper.
The gut, raw, that cannot be peeled away.
It will not do, it will not do.

These days, sunburned inside out,
a bouquet of dried roses stuck in my throat
prickles every ampule
of swallowed tears.

JULIA'S SCARF
(for Jill)

We have unrealized seeds in us,
and in cancer-crisis, they launch
tendrils of pure goodness,
but instead of reaching for sunlight,
they reach for me.

Once, pre-cancer, I met Julia Child
at the sink in the ladies room of LaGuardia.
She trilled hello with gusto.
I bowed to her.
I cherish that moment with the melodious goddess of butter.

When I shed my hair,
Jill made an offering to me,
a gift from Julia to her,
a cherished memento, passed down to my Jill.
A token of Jill's and Julia's friendship.
A scarf.

I say no.

I still cannot imagine Julia's silk
insulating my fuzzy head
without crying.

It's not the scarf.

It's the possibility of it.

The bountiful sacrifice,
the noble offer of this precious treasure.
It encircles and blankets me
with sustenance.

GOIN' TO WALMART WITH MY PARTY DRESS ON
(thanks for the lift, Tena!)

Cancer is a crazy pass.
Like you wake up one morning without nausea
(Finally! Yee-haw!)
and you almost guffaw at your husband
(trying to sleep 10 more minutes, how dare he on this of all days),
I'm goin' to Walmart in my party dress!
He eyebrows you like Spock, tests your forehead for cancer fever.

You rumba to your closet and gussy-up
in your favorite Maria von Trapp party dress –
pleated and cotton and bow at the hips and –
you git yourself a ride to Walmart.

You don't care if everyone stares at you
lookin' like Elly May Clampett at the prom.
Heck, you already have cancer!
Nothing can dampen your style now.

And tomorrow?
Maybe a whimsical waltz to the mailbox.
An email blast of Valentines to your friends
(it's not Valentine's Day, but you knew that).
A tea party on the lawn in the rain.

Go ahead, stare and wonder.
I have cancer! I'm living. Join me.

MARY SUNSHINE
(for M.C.)

I am a pacifist.
But some things are worth the fight.
Like a friendship.
Like the time we used words to wound each other so deeply
I could taste blood in my mouth.
It was you who clawed through the debris
and swooped to my front door in tears to rescue us.
You taught me how to surrender my heavy, heavy ego.
Because sometimes this life is hard to navigate alone.
And you were right.
Years later, you cradled me the moment the word cancer invaded.

You and I have unfinished business.
Riding the roller coaster at Santa's Village.
Sneaking off to movies while our kids are at school.
Walking the dogs in the snow.

Some things are worth fighting for.
The promise of your cheerful voice no matter what.
This life. With you.

GOOD TIMING
(for Geetanjali)

If our children had been born in a different year.
If we had not a mutual friend in Joy (so aptly named).
If you'd preferred the ocean to country living.
If you'd been a dentist instead of a G.I.

Luckily for me, God lobbed all of these possibilities
into a serendipitous juggling act,
and converged them, intersecting our coordinates
like dust and straw swirling down a dirt road
to form a perfect tumbleweed.

My life is balanced by your being, dear friend.
Most literally, good doctor, my life is by your being.

NEED
(for George)

Cancer can make you fall in love again.
The daily love has been there –
you know what I mean? –
ensuring the quotidian care of each other,
clean pressed shirts, a paycheck, groceries,
meals, New Year's Eve champagne,
a welcome bed, and on and on.

But then comes cancer,
slapping you in the face one day,
and instead of weeping solo in a cold rain,
he is there beside you,
holding you for dear life,
sitting at your feet with the dog,
shadowing you, willing you faith,
and suffering long days of chemicals pumping
through your veins, giving you brain-muscle
to cope with this awful cancer,
and you know he would take the needle himself,
and you are grateful it is you not him
who has to suffer the physical,
and he tells you how beautiful
your shaved head looks, meaning it,
and he touches your hand,
and that is plenty.

WAITING FOR SURGERY

Is this what God intended?
A punctured abdomen,
mottled with incisions
like an apple pelted by hail

a body empty of tissues
that abandoned their purpose
to breed cancer

As you brace yourself for slicing,
you sincerely hope
this is God's plan

You tell yourself your surgeon
is a sculptor of innards,
a master of creation

You know your family is
not as strong as you
when your father died young

You recall the gypsy fortune teller who,
pointing to your life line,
traced her papery finger down, down,
your youthful palm,
promising, promising

You pluck hope from all of this
and hold on to it for dear life

RULES OF FORGETTING

In the beginning was the word cancer,
slicing your lifeline in half with stainless steel
precision.
You greet your morning self in bathroom mirror daily,
like a Muslim facing east,
thank God for the day.
There is no forgetting the present hemisphere.
It's prickly, but it is.
You do not take it for granted.

It's the other hemisphere you need
to lop off and swat away.
Forget the way it was.

> last runner's high, bellyful of warm salty popcorn, good red wine swirling in crystal glass, 31 flavors, the sound of your own singing, sleeping with head on flat pillow, cradling your fetal body into his

These words are the remains.
They stick in your craw like bony fish,
like claws.
Swallow.

FEAR OF FAILURE

Chemotherapy doesn't come with a warranty.
Ditto radiation, surgery.
Every three months you await scan results,
slap away bad thoughts like whack-a-moles.
Impatiently poised, your hand hovers over
tissue box, recalling childhood Ouija,
waiting for movement in any direction.

The first time the good news comes
you flood your eyes, raise them to God,
move your lips, inaudibly thank Him,
let your doctor clasp your hand in hers.

This is an equalizing moment,
the power of good news leveling the see-saw.
Not like the bad first time, when it tipped you
on your head, away, away
from control.

You open your arms to temporary steadiness.
What else can you do

GET OVER THIS GIRL

Look out.
I'm a splinter in your soft sole.
I'm the taste of copper in your mouth.
The cancer took the girl you fell in love with.
It will come back for me in a black Corvette.
I will drape myself in red for our love, sweet.
Wear something white to clean your slate
like a plated good meal.
Lick your lips, savor new love.
Save yourself.

CANCER BUDDIES
(for Lois)

Friend, you pull your sweater taut over new breasts.
Size D. You deliver the news sheepishly,
like a bad report card to parents,
whisper with schoolgirl embarrassment
of your trip to the bra store to harness them.

I am envious.

Not of your suffering. Nor of your girls.
That you resurfaced after cancer still whole, newly minted, not worn away.

Friend, I tug my loose waistband.
Not much goes down my lopped-off throat anymore.
Facing mortality every day wears me down as well.

If we could snap a wishbone perfectly,
push the halves back together, merge.

RECURRENCE
(for B.C.)

It's not yours.
But it might as well be.
The cancer bully is back at you,
taunting and shoving itself in your face with bad news.
Calling you a sucker.
This time, a child.
It shouldn't be about you, but it is.
Fear and nausea bubble up and spill out.
You know the child's body will buck at the chemical surges.
You know the child's brain will balk at what the body will be asked to do.
You know the child's pain will be fierce.
Worse.
You know the mother's pain will be wild.
The word cancer bores into you,
deeper than a diagnosis this time,
a rabid assault on a mother's power to shelter.
His cancer is your cancer.
Her sorrow, ours.
Yet we rise from bed, move through the house,
grip the day with two hands,
stare it down.

PARADOX
(for B.C.)

Cancer begins with voiding.
Child, you give up pieces of yourself, a Lenten sacrifice.
Slough off cells, scoop out masses,
accept the sterile poison into your veins.

What a miracle of faith you are,
squirting your parents' future grandkids into a cup,
banking on love.
Oh, how we will dance at your wedding one day.

Today, we woo the angels near you,
reach for God's hand and pull him towards you.

GUILTING THE LILY
(in loving memory of Mary Downing)

You are terminal.

Here is a story for us:
Two girls, stone soup poor, moving in tandem
mothered by crazies in the sixties
near the sneaker factory.
I blame our cancers on those smokestacks.
My conspiracy theory, chemicals percolated by free choice in a fallen world.
I cannot blame God.
The bad timing that plopped us into East Watertown
is the good timing that swirled us together.
And drove us to get the hell out of there.

My cancer should have killed me already,
yours, swathed in soft pink satin,
swished you into survivor walkathons.
What happened?

It's not my story yet.
My husband will still hold me at night,
my children call Mom and catch my answer.
I am grateful for that, the kind of grateful
That drops me to my knees daily.

Today I let the train carry me to face you one last time.
Drooping with shame, I will rub your feet with lotion,
pump your hand with mine, pray if you'll let me,
ask for strength and good painkillers, comfort.

Don't look for sense in the ending,
only love, cutting through the fog.
The white of this page says it all.

MARY, MARY

Remember Lynda Carter, that smoky beauty from the 70s, Wonder Woman?
Mary, Mary, your staccato laugh ricocheted off walls like bullets off her gold cuffs
every time we gushed your resemblance.

It's been nearly 40 years.
Your beauty radiates, even in cancer, even in ashes.

I'll be honest: this is a struggle.
It's more than writer's block, the tugging and wrenching of vowels,
like kids talking underwater, the crispy sounds elusive and stale.
Maybe a painter could better conjure your light and lilt.

I have failed you before.
When you slipped into your life, away,
plopped into the pillowy world, arms outstretched.
I was not there.
I'm so sorry for missing, missing those wonder years with you.

Mary, Mary, you opened your arms to me like the grace of a new day,
Mary, Mary, my mantra, as if chanting your name will bring you to my side,
laughing and swearing.

And here I am missing you all over again.

Today in Provincetown we'll gather our words like broken shells,
swallow down our sorrow, make joy from memory.
Beautiful woman, I'm trying to lasso the goodness you scattered in your wake
before it dissipates like dust, but truth is:
the world is not better without you.

WHAT I WANT YOU TO KNOW

There is no cure for my cancer.
That may explain my perspective:
peripheral tunnel vision.

I have lost my palette, ice-cream,
a hearty meal, gourmet everything.
But not the first sip of hot, strong,
French-pressed coffee in the morning.
I cling to my cup fiercely.
Don't bother me then.

I have lost my patience for sponge-friends –
the ones who suck your spirit and wring you out –
the ones bloated with self-absorption.
I am weary of their whining,
and this tortured metaphor.
I turn from them with a leaden heart,
wish them well, like a castaway
chucking the last bottle to sea.

I have lost a good night's sleep.
Forever.
Get it?
I wonder what it was like to lie flat.
To spoon like a young woman in love.

I have not lost my sense of humor,
I delight in the ridiculous.
When my doctor trumpets,
Your colon is clean; see you in 10 years,
I nearly flop with laughter:
No more colonoscopies!

omG, did I say that out loud?
Sometimes I do.
Not for shock value.
Just keeping perspective between the lines,
expectations in check.

Know there is no evidence of cancer within me
Today that technology can detect.
And wow, if I can say that a decade from now,
I will guzzle that prep like a pirate and eat these words!

I have lost 25 pounds.
And I get as annoyed with you when you mourn
your loss of self-control after a full plate of pasta,
as you with me for my failure to fill a size 00.

I have gained friendships richer than
chocolate fudge, wider than rainforest canopies.
And faith, stronger than Hollywood superheroes,
Sitting on my shoulder, poking me with possibility –
A cure? A miracle? Winning lottery ticket?
Or a simple gift:
Here is another day for you. Look!

HEALING

I am voyeur now.
An old movie.
Extra in the crowd scene periphery.
Blurred on the edges.
In Santa Monica, son, I felt your pull
to the ocean, wriggle my hand from your fingers.
I can't save you so I watch,
Pumice my feet with sand.
I know I should be grateful to be here,
and I am, truly I am, but I swear I can still feel the chunks that cancer took,
phantom aches, and I will my body to rhyme the wave with a curve.

YOUR SIX WORD STORY

"For sale: Baby shoes. Never worn."
-- Ernest Hemingway

My son laughed at this one.
Not wanting to belabor the tragedy,
I explained the un-joke, pithy and somber.
Loving parents. Baby wanted. Never born.
Oh, he said. *I thought the baby refused to wear the shoes.*

My turn to laugh.

My hopeful storyline for his lineage:
Mix laughter with good wishes: Blissings.

GARBAGE TOWN

[Manshiet Nasser, Cairo – largest Christian church in Middle East, constructed in garbage dump. See photographs by Carsten Snejberg.]

Cast-offs sift filth, exhuming treasures from trash,
creating selves, specialist dealers in tin, plastic, wood,
the unwanted.

Economies rise from the mounds,
salvagers collect & recycle,
collect & recycle,
collect & recycle.

Even here, boys shoot pool, addicts shoot up.
Even here, girls marry in white.
Schools, faith, rise from exile.

We take it all into our lenses,
afraid to touch the living,
grapple with their comfort.

Even here, there are rich.
One says, "This is life for me."
This place, teeming with refuse.

II.

GETTING PAST WORDS AGAIN

It is mostly the unsaid
that must be precisely observed with a jeweler's loop, disciplined,
queued up like a line of cocaine before a slapstick sneeze trumpets chaos.

Checklist:
Eye contact: no
Paper shuffling: yes
Sound: no

No sound.

Before "not good" and "cancer" welt your face, already wet,
you have already known.
Before the words breathe,
you cannot explain the way the unsaid tines scooped your gut raw.

"Not what we want to tell you…"

You watch the words trail over your shoulder,
try to catch them like 3D images, wrangle air,
catch your husband's eye, grab his arm for balance though you're sitting.

There is only wailing, like widows in old-country black cotton,
wailing down the street for lost babies, *my babies, my babies*.

The words are black ink on crisp black linen, darker than death.
Death is peace in the arms of angels.
The light of God on your lips.
The words herald suffering, precurse.

I'M PISSED OFF

Today another movie star shot up with heroin for the last time and I have to admit I am beyond miffed because here I sit propped up in my old lady chair my veins pulsing with a different poison, the kind that needs to lasso a miracle meanwhile Philip Seymour Hoffman oh my how grand three names tossed himself in the gutter of his fancy schmancy NY apt with kids loving kids down the street probably and I would give anything, almost anything, to slap that stupid man hard and ask *what the hell were you thinking you ungrateful piece of Hollywood shit to turn away from all this*

NEW LOVE SONG FOR THE OLD
(Happy Valentine's Day 2014 to George from Margaret)

I saw them again the other day.
The crinkles at the sides of your eyes, concentric half-moons,
like the rings orbiting the heart of a tree.
It meant you were smiling. I could only see your profile, but I know the signs.
Oh, love, how I fell for those lines years ago, rings ago.
I miss them already.

You may be wondering, why start a love song by a dying
woman with such quotidian intimacy.

And then there is the way you tilt your head to my shoulder when we sit side-by-side. It was easier when there was flesh instead of cancer bone, but the sentiment remains, like some Vulcan primordial attempt to mind meld, pre-vocal. As if to say I am made to love you and I you. There are no barriers to love at these molecular levels.

There is the steel-hard concentration on math you insist on for fun,
the devotion to snowsledding with our son, running my fingers through your hair without complaint, patience, impatience (for life is complicated). All joy to me, voyeur, cataloguer.

I spend too much love-energy worrying. Are you eating? Is your car safe?
Are your clothes clean? Dentist? Eye doctor? Vitamins? I keep the lists.
Annoyance erupts when checks go unchecked. You look past that.

I keep the lists small and large. The way one morning you bent over toward me in the kitchen to pop open your shirt pocket and reveal a ring, feigning gasped surprise. *Cartier.* Three bands intertwined, kinetic. Fresh strawberries on the bedside table. Gazing at the Renoir dancers, nearly in tears at the raw beauty, feeling their swing as my heart swooned so close to you in the gallery.

There is the way you open your arms to me and let me in, full embrace.

That's all there is, *love.*

STRAWBERRIES IN THE MAILBOX
(for A.S.)

Someone is building a nest in my mailbox.
It started with strawberries the day cancer hissed back at me.
The trinkets arrive *sotto voce*.
I remove them, assemble them, rearrange,
let the juiciness of the tender fruits drip down my chin.

Some days it's magazines, *People*, British tabloids, even an *MIT Review*
(ha ha ha, I am a poet, so this is quite funny and the laugh feels delicious).
One day, an old fruit basket filled with smooth rocks,
each one hand-etched with the word love.
A prayer shawl knit by local churchwomen. A Valentine.

People sigh with helplessness, mouths parched for words.
The truth is this: we are as resourceful as birds building nests.
The empty mailbox beckons.
The red flag up, like a painted fingernail, a siren call, a beacon, come look, come see.
I scoop up the small offerings, so generous for my heart's sparrow's place
in this world, say a prayer for the givers.
Thank you, God, for a large suburban mailbox, a vessel to collect the blessings.

FIDELITY
(for K.P.C.)

I woke up to a memory.

Feet balanced on the deck rail altar, Sunday paper smudged on my fingers, you
making an offering of coffee.
The woods, a squirrel stopping to watch me, suspicious, as if he knew
how temporary the light was at that moment, what Monet knew and taught us,
that what we see changes.

I'm dying now and I tell you what I have said before,
that I have always loved you, even when I didn't,
even when the chunk of cruelty lodged deep in my heart
slammed a baseball through our canvas.
Maybe that's where the cancer started.

This morning I look to the impasse of snow that brakes my way
to the patio in a different house.
My fingers tap feeble words that limp across the backlit page.
Upstairs, my husband sleeps.
Yes, I love him.
Upstairs, my son.
There is the disconnect: I'm in a sorry state but even you would not begrudge
the wonder of boy barely visible under a mound of stuffed bears that rise and fall
to his breathing.

I give inadequate apology, as I fuss over these globs of words.
Know this: I leave you a trophy of love's shape shifting,
love's nugget, our daughter, the promise.

PATIENT

People tell me how brave I am.
I tell them God has not given me a choice.

There are children who need me to ping back like sonar when they call my name.
A man helplessly in love.
Friends whirling 'round me like electrons to my nucleus.
They are all in this world.
Only something very strong can break those bonds.

That is why I rise each morning.
Take the needle. Surrender vanity and wear the skullcap in public. Wait.

And when my body bucks at being told what to do
I wait.
For pills to release relief to the body, for cells to grow, for cells to die.

Do not mistake love for bravery,
love stubborn as the weary child at bedtime
clinging to day.

NOT WILLIAM, NOT CAROLINE

I am waiting for my name to be called in the room full of others
whose bodies have been hijacked by cancer
when the nurse calls out, "*William*."
That single word corsets my breath.
My son, my daughter, may you never hear your name called like that.

LETTING GO

I'm driving and the sky fills my windshield,
stunned that God's glorious world on earth will go on without me.
It's humbling: the self-importance I tout in making my family's days
is sleight of hand, momentary illusion.
Now you see me, now you don't.

Who will make my son's breakfast, ensure his winter boots fit every year?
Who will plan my daughter's wedding, embrace my grandchildren,
make my husband laugh, comfort friends bruised by life?
Someone.

These trees will continue to shed snow, cradle nests,
my house will welcome friends, even this car will outlast my body.
This is why I write. To stay tethered to you.

AFFINITIES
(for A.S.)

I look to God for sustenance.
But there are side dishes.
Here is a story about my friend:
She searched for her Native American spirit guides and found a bear.
Imagine the balance of silent meditation with a snarling bear roaring
in one's mind, growling orders, Go out and seize your life, woman.
She did.
Then, years later, again, the bear roams back into her mind,
a cub, nuzzling her into the softening of motherhood, peace.

I admit, I love this story.

I took an online test to find my Native American spirit guides,
expecting God to reveal a wounded bird.
Instead, I am swan. And wolf.
Dreamer. Fighter.

Yesterday, resting, I heard noise at the front door.
My dog, lovingly cared for by neighborhood friends
escaped and charged back to me.
I guess he raced two miles to find his way here,
through snarled woods and spring slush,
a long way for little legs, little dog.
He considered me through the glass door, front paws poised
waiting, as if to say,
Phew. You're still here. Let me in.

There is something within us all to guide.

DIVERSIONS

I have been scheming,
a sorcerer hunched over a cauldron,
rubbing hands together in sly delight
as I shift my friends into place
like chess maneuvers.
In this analogy, I am the one in check.

My friends, when I am gone,
you will need someone to hold you
as friends, as daughters do.

There is my Margie, my Mary,
in the same picture frame now
in my kitchen, side-by-side,
connecting like new neuronal pathways
when discoveries are made.
We are all three laughing as you tell each other the stories I already know.

I imagine your telling the new story,
the story of how your friend, Margaret, nudged you into the same orbit.

HOLES IN THE HEART

My son will have a big hole in his little lamb of a heart when I'm gone.
That's what my friend, Jilly, said. And she is right.
He and I are squirreling away tidbits for emergency patching.
The unsolicited kiss on small boy's orb of cheek,
bread-baking lessons, noticing God in the moments.
Nibbles of me to snack on to fill the void.

Then there is you, daughter.
Your hole is already deep and black,
festering and suspicious, like a bull before rodeo mounting.
Like late dives from sleep, springing upright into dark
to shake off nightmare willies.
Like regret that worms around your throat until.

I do not understand it, the anger you claw and snort at me.
I stare you down with mother love.
Hope for a day you can open your hands like dove wings,
launch yourself to someone who will boomerang back a direct hit.

I pray I would be present for the mending,
but this cancer is eating its own holes in my bones even as I write this.
You will need to reach into crevices, reach for crumbs in the sofa,
feel for me with faith.
You will find me, skulking around, knowing I love you always, even now.

SIGNS

The thing about dying Christians is the wonder
and the wondering.
Will you know, my loves, my presence?
Will I?

Will there be good cooking shows? Can I savor the concoctions?
What about the smell of mud? Or my son's shampooed hair?
Will I finally learn to ski?

Will God sprinkle some me-spirit into the hawks in my yard so I can watch,
or weave me into the grass under your bare feet when you run to catch the Frisbee?

Will you feel me reach out and breathe on your shoulder at the beach on a
still and sunny day?
When you remember the laughs at my kitchen counter, will I laugh too?

When Judy Garland croons our song in the elevator, on the radio in the restaurant,
will it be dj'd by me?
When you reach for my phantom body in the early morning, will it still be warm?

Or is it more direct? Will I counsel you when you least expect it?
Will you hear voices?
*Don't buy those shoes. No, that avocado there instead. You must read this book.
Brush your teeth.*

Or maybe it's even deeper. The compass in your soul that tells you whom to
marry, where to settle and why, when to quit, and when to try harder?

You will need to look for the signs,
gather them in your arms like autumn's rogue leaves,
like inviting the snow to fall on your upturned face,
like the slosh through Gloucester's cold ocean waves to scoop the sea glass,
heart-shaped rocks, trinkets tossed back to shore.

You will need faith then as much as I do now.

CHARLES STREET REPAIRS

The rule should be cancer trumps all other hardship,
strong-arming out the mundane dents in a day,
broken appliances and mismatched socks, dust on the piano,
those time-suck chores and obligations that lurch the days forward.

But that's not the way it is.
In my microcosm Skelly world (think cartoon-like frail bird pajama-clad
50-something lady shuffling through glass house observing and tidying)
things break beside my bones.
Socks go missing.
Then reappear under sofas, clogging the vacuum.
Dust settles and thickens and, yes, annoys me.
Ditto the road construction that surfaces every queasy morning
at the Charles Street exit while I sludge my way toward treatment.
A little break here?

Here is how I repair.
First, the look-back:
closed eyes, whiff of *Chanel No. 5*, courtship walks on Charles Street,
back of your hand shyly brushing mine, stopping to pause,
hands to each other's faces, espresso on your breath, considering
the thrill of building a life of unknown, unfathomable content.
That memory is still ripe with satisfaction.
Things were broken then, yes, but there was no cancer.

Next, hammer out the chinks of the day.
Tap out ribbons of unsolicited "I love you" texts.
Some recipients will catch their breath with fear illness has exploded,
lower their head to hide burning red cheeks, or tears, but most will :)
or LOL and forget about this world's burdens for a moment or longer.
Some may save the pixel chain for a booster shot.

I guess it's all about perspective.
The long tow rope that tugs us forward does blister the hands.
Along the way, savor chunks of memory, a latte and salve.

THANK YOU, MRS. FLOWERS
(A Tribute to Maya Angelou)

Voice rich as fine espresso, you spoke
only when goaded by Mrs. Flowers
who cupped you in her hands,
cuddled your marvelous brain back into being
after unspeakable childhood horror
that severed your voice for years.
You wrote, instead.
Her simple words: "Child, don't tell me you love poetry.
You don't love poetry. You have to speak poetry to love it."
Thank you, Mrs. Flowers.

I don't presume to know why the caged bird sings.
My life tragedies mute next to yours, poet Queen.
You speak even now, and I will not hear of a world that silences you.

As I sit here, mumbling through my own humble verses
of cancer and love and faith
I do know this truth: rare wild flowers reach through roadside debris,
quiet beauty rises from sorrow-soaked ashes,
and, yes, the caged bird does sing sugary notes that bounce from hope to hope
like bees jitterbugging from posy to posy.
Listen.

ON NOT BEING GOOD ENOUGH MOST DAYS

Yesterday, melancholy, as I loved my garden from my resting chair inside.
Fed up with mosquitoes feeding on my ankles,
from behind a glass wall I admired the now carpet of vinca,
dubiously and painfully planted years ago in pathetic clumps.
Funny how we take so much and so little on faith.
The vinca will conquer your dirt with green, splashed with purple, like a Pollock.
We greedily drank in our scruffy landscaper's prophecy.

My doctors tell me there's always something they can do.
That's a little harder to stomach on faith alone.
Show me the numbers, open your data to me, parade out the people who still live.
Is there a catalogue? Cancer patients who thrive in Zone 6?
Do they have names?

Like the vinca, the cancer will tendril out, but weedy and wicked.
What to do? I can manage only the smallest of gestures.
Worry about my cholesterol.
Savor Mercer's delicious eggs anyway.
Snuggle the dog that steadfastly refuses to move from my chair
even as I lower my bum millimeters from his stubborn coat.
Experiment with lavender in plum pie I cannot eat.
Tell you I love you at every opportunity, schmaltz or not.

I will miss all this.
Some days, I miss it already.
My little failures – forgetting birthdays, what you told me an hour ago,
sarcasm, advice honest as a hornet's nest, tearing up and losing hope –
forgive me on an ongoing basis.
Please. It's only temporary.

Plants do not have a central nervous system.
They reach deep to suck the soil's nutrients, survival maneuvers,
not instinct like babies' tender mouths rooting for mom.
I'm looking out my window again.
Time to plant a project.
Planning annuals for my children to soak in the garden's promise of renewal.

FRIENDS AND SHIPS

I have always had a hard time letting go.
Of arguments, of cherished clothes from the – *gulp* – '80s,
of books, CDs, even vinyl, shoes, and most of all, people.

I wouldn't say my hardship rises to the level of hoarding
but I will admit to saving letters, rubber bands,
pulling friends close to my heart long after friendship has sizzled,
festering a recipe of ½ anger, ½ tears when the adhesive snaps.

It's my exhausting impracticality of trying to hold onto the absolute glint
of bestness that everyone radiates from their daily beings,
like God's light from a prism.

Of course, sometimes it's my fault, and I slink away. Then there is guilt.

Don't get me wrong: it doesn't happen often, but geography, professions,
families and hobbies can cast bumpy waves and throw us off course.
It just is.

But here is what I have learned through crisis:
friends are like ships in a regatta,
runners in a marathon at the edge of a terror-bombed finish line.
They rally with colorful flags, they offer a steady arm. Some do.
Many do. Or wish they could.
And even communicating that wish is enough to fill my sail most days.

And here is something else truly remarkable that I have learned:
Often our ocean of friends regenerates, a magnificent blessing
that on this day of my 52nd birthday I cherish and nuzzle.
New friends. Renewed friendships. Even at my age.

Like finding a penny, turning it in our fingers,
getting to know its glimmer in the sunshine,
or hugging the comfort of lost change found jingling in an old pocket,
or delighting in the thrill of tossing coins into water with a wish.
As if to say, *I am so grateful to find you.*
Winking back.

ON MAUI

I rise in darkness each morning here
to watch the sun from my lanai ease out of the horizon
and illuminate the water, verdant hills.

I need its heat now more than ever to warm my bones
on this, my farewell tour, family in tow,
etching landscapes and portraits into their memories,
that can pull them toward me when I am no longer.

It's like the tides, really.
Waves reach for the shore from the Pacific calm at the vanishing point
and break at my ankles. Rewind. Repeat. Remember.

These are days of unimaginable sadness and beauty,
more exquisite than the red hibiscus, bowing in embarrassment at its own elegance,
the sprawling banyan caged by cement, the sacred stories of immigrant workers,
grateful to exchange poverty for subsistence on this island.
Here, at least they have choice.

And when I think about it that way, so do I.
Dying, or living on Maui?
Letting go or holding tight?
It's hard not to pluck optimism from a tropical paradise.
To turn the eye outward, not inward at the cancer that creeps through my bones.
To hoist off the woe of not returning here.
To grab the warmth of sun with hungry fist, unpalm it to my cheek.
To greet the morning with greed.

REUNION

For brother's 70th birthday, a reunion of those stitched to his heart:
Children, grandchildren, siblings, and a new, welcome outcrop,
called to Cape Cod to cull stories from our memory banks
like kernels from the cob, and pop them open like fireworks.

Why is it so hard to voice the unsaid without occasion,
like speaking God's name, or naming the Tao,
to crack open the heart and spill it out like a tsunami?
I mean the L word, released in a flood of tribute and a clink of flutes.

We celebrate George's goodness, nod to our own dents and fissures,
patting down misgivings with all there is, love, forgiveness, love.
We are each other's glue.
I guess that's how it is with families, even those whose
imperfections poke out along the way, break off, sanded down, repair.

Wired to each other like rickety wagon wheels that keep the cart going,
I gathered in the stories of a loving father I did not really know,
whose disease, like mine, was sudden as whiplash,
the stories of brothers leaning into each other when life got too damned hard.

It's not all platters of melancholy and bowls of mushed tears, of course.

There is humor, but I am not funny. If I were, I could recount for you here
the hilarious stories told that day, and you would laugh
until you cried, as did I, wanting more.

I am thankful to have them, even as I listened and realized my own absence
from many of the stories, even as I understood solemnly that I would be absent again,
but rear up in the stories some day notwithstanding, like my own father.

There is the astounding magic of DNA,
the blueprint of spunk and soft hair like sunshine
in Connor and Ronin, Caroline and William,
that crossed oceans, American plains, smudged city streets,
and wriggles its way through, a glint in the eye.

Tell me more.

LAUGH TRACK

Remember canned laughter from 70's sitcoms,
the quips that don't quite rise to cream of the comedy
but trigger an audience guffaw anyway?

That's how it is some days with cancer as my soundtrack.

Science prescribes daily laughter. Seriously.
So every day it is my son's job to tell me a joke.
I laugh, if only at the pureness of his yummy delight.

He always belly-laughs at his own humor, and that's exactly how it should be,
like the dog chasing its tail, a one-guy tour-de-force.

It's not easy.
Sometimes his jokes are, well, un-funny, to me.
Especially the ones involving physics,
that I, frankly, do not get.
Being an English major and all.

And there are days I'd rather cry, and I do.
But here's what I have learned:
pathos does not inspire, it smothers and dims a day.

I swear that if I swallowed my son I'd glow like a harvest moon,
and bounce down the street with a bellyful of balloons.
So, heartfelt or labored, I gulp down his banquet of jokes to remind me: heal.

CELLS

Most of us on the 7th floor of Yawkey have tunnel-worry.
We focus our energy and hope to shrink cells,
think mini ray guns like video game tools blasting cancer.

Today in line at the head and neck cancer check in counter,
an anomaly to begin with, because my broken cells are not in my head
or my neck, a beautiful woman, round at the belly, is before me.

Another anomaly.

My brain cannot conceive how her body knows which cells to conquer,
and which to divide.
Does the globule of baby in her belly nudge against a tumor, kick at nausea,
or just bob like a buoy in a wave, trusting?

The woman turns, smiles at me.
I want to take her arm, guide her to maternity, another building.
Anywhere but here.
I want to cleave from Yawkey today myself, run like Marvel's Flash,
this chemo day.
Instead, I will this woman iron muscle, ray guns like bazookas,
and a boy, or a girl.

I think of my own babies.
It doesn't matter if the bucket of cells we love is on the outside or inside.
The will to fight is the same.

VULNERABILITY
(for L.W.)

It's assuming snow angel position like a yoga pose,
falling backwards into the cloud
knowing the ice flakes will sift into your boot tops and chill you,
sinking into winter froth anyway.

It's waiting for the whammy,
ticking through each day with whiplash emotions:
I'm here, now! But I'm so scared.
Will I be surprised today by the genius of a good book?
An early burst of New England fall's red, orange, and yellow clusters?
Or a mystery ache needing attention and worrybeads and a universe of prayer?

It's wanting to cruise the Mediterranean like a kid wants candy,
to soak in more of this world dripping with gooey delish.
It's wanting to stay in the daily routine of predictable comforts instead,
make toast, drink tea, treasure the baby snapping turtles crossing cement to their
mamas, cherished routines stitched together over a lifetime.

Either way, it's a longing infused with terror and glee,
spinning yin and yang into a powerful tornado that
can drop a house on the bad, or our heads, or port a good pair of shoes to our feet.

Let's take the shoes, my friend. In red.

TURNING CORNERS

There is an art to making a bed,
folding sheets like paper airplanes, turning
crisp hospital corners.
Some argue, what is the point of making a bed
when it will be unmade again?
I iron the sheets, breathe rising warm steam,
peel and tuck.

I am edgy with every ache these days,
conjuring fantastic evil stories of my demise.
Last week stabbing pain in my tonsil
catapulted me to the hospital in a storm of weary tears.
This week, the aching hip, nagging like a mother,
lures me to internet medical frights.
I am like the gal in a horror movie,
short-changed on common sense and swollen with impulse,
terrified of what lurks in the basement of my bones.

So I make the bed, nostalgic for middle school home economics class,
dainty sewing, lessons in linens.

When sleep hauls me to bed,
I am grateful for the day.
And when I rise,
I am grateful for the day.

HOLDING ELIZA

It's a high,
cheek to teeny fuzzy scalp,
inhaling yummy baby scent,
sugar cookies and vanilla bean.

My own baby girl hugs like a zombie now,
shoulder to shoulder tap,
mumbling heart you with a mouthful of pebbles,
eyes down or away.
Some days I nourish maternal love with mere happy-face
tweets and texts.

But I'll take it, daughter.
I am still addicted to you,
even after teetering on the rocky edge of teen world,
stuck in a one-legged yoga pose I could barely hold.
You are chocolate espresso cake, Chanel No. 5,
squirming into womanhood without me.

I wish a magic spell to stop the clock,
a holding pattern.

I DIDN'T DO ANYTHING WRONG

We've been trained to look for blame.
Smoking causes cancer.
But I have never smoked.

I ran long distances for a healthy high,
my heart beating so slowly alarms chirped an ironic warning
during a routine screening.
I sneak a peak at my Boston Marathon finisher medal
from time to time
like a toppled princess may stroke her jewels in the secret darkness of her closet.

I ate my vegetables, pushed animals from my plate, drank only red wine
in moderation.

I steered through my days like an Indy 500 driver turned tight corners,
in supreme control.

Yet here I sit, upright, unable to lie down,
with a midget esophagus and a Barbie-sized stomach,
fasting to ward off complications, distress.

I was warned with the first diagnosis: do not be an angry victim.
And most days I graciously co-exist with mutant cells
that sprout like pesky weeds in my body.
Still, I wonder.

Why did this cancer choose me as its host?
Why are my bones eroding?

Sometimes there is no answer in this life.

RAINBOW HAIKUS

Morning of good news:
no progression of disease.
Thank you, thank you, God.

Lifting eyes in praise,
a chunk of rainbow in clouds
startles me to tears.

MENISCUS IN THE BEAKER

["When water is placed in a glass or plastic container the surface takes on a curved shape. This curve is known as a meniscus. Volumetric glassware is calibrated such that reading the bottom of the meniscus, when it is viewed at eye level, will give accurate results. Viewing the meniscus at any other angle will give inaccurate results." -- http://www.harpercollege.edu/tmps/chm/100/dgodambe/ thedisk/labtech/volume.htm]

Chemistry, like baking, like writing, commands precision.
When measuring liquids, one must scooch
to eye level with the beaker,
examine the concave line where liquid bumps air,
and assay its accuracy
against the forefront of graduated, but arbitrary, really, lines.
And record a judgment.

What I mean by this is God did not dictate the metric system,
or chemical equations, but
what I mean is that we sway and bend in a universe of rules
that nonetheless pull us on track enough most days,
like magnetized train wheels,
or is it the magnetized track?

It's like that throughout my days,
living and dying with cancer.
How to judge the moment,
how to cast it – bronze, silver, gold?

Sometimes it's clear as H20.
Like when my son and I give wiggly hugs before bed,
grasping each other and jiggling like ancient washing machine agitators.
But we are the opposite of agitated.
Sometimes it's murky, like news of scans that show lesions and tumors,
lurking in my body, just being for now.

We sway and bend,
hands in the air, surrendering to the best part of the ride, the swoon,
the dizzy, downward, upward, rollercoaster swoon
that ends with a giddy whee!

NOTES

Made in the USA
Middletown, DE
06 March 2015